11+
Verbal Reasoning
GL & Other Styles

TESTBOOK 5

Standard & Multiple-choice 6 Minute Tests

Dr Stephen C Curran

Edited by Autumn McMahon

This book belongs to

Accelerated Education Publications Ltd

Guidance notes for parents

These tests can be completed as standard or multiple-choice tests.

Multiple-choice Tests

Answers are entered onto the answer sheets at the back of the book. The actual test would be marked by a computer but, for the purposes of these practice tests, you will need to mark it yourself. It is important for your child to treat it like the real thing and record an answer in the appropriate box by drawing a clear line through their chosen box with a pencil. Mistakes should be carefully rubbed out and not crossed out since in the actual test this would not be correctly recorded by the computer.

Standard Tests

Ask your child to fill in all the answers in the spaces as instructed in each section. Mistakes should be crossed through with a single line and the correct answer written clearly.

Marking and Feedback

The answers are provided at the back of this book. Only these answers are allowed. One mark should be given for each correct answer. Do not deduct marks for wrong answers. Do not allow half marks or 'the benefit of the doubt', as this might mask a child's need for extra help in the topic and does not replicate the real exam conditions. Always try to be positive and encouraging. Talk through any mistakes with your child and work out together how to arrive at the right answer.

Verbal Reasoning Test 1

1) The word inside the brackets has been formed in the same way as the example given. Write the missing word.

   UNTIE (CHANT) BEACH   ALERT (_____) CLASH

2) Write the number which will complete the sum.

   $3 \times 9 + 8 = 60 \div 4 +$ _____

3) The middle number in the last group is made in the same way as the middle numbers in the first two groups. Find the missing number. (____)

   (8 [57] 7) (6 [49] 8)
   (9 [____] 7)

4) Write the three-letter word that will complete the word in bold type.

   Mixing chemicals can cause a dangerous **REION**.   (_____)

5) Three of the four words below are given in code. The codes are not written in the same order as the words and one code is missing.

   HAZE   ZERO   THEM   MARE

   4281   5314   6187

   Find the code for **RAZOR**.   (_____)

6) Move one letter from the first word and place it into the second word to make two new words. Write the letter.

   RUGBY   LOVE   (____)

7) Underline two words, one from each set of brackets, which are most similar in meaning.

   (brash, boost, boast)   (brag, brake, brisk)

8) Complete this analogy by underlining one word from each set of brackets.

   Match is to (wood, contest, fire) as **rich** is to (money, spend, wealthy)

9) If **A = 4**, **B = 8**, **C = 16**, **D = 12** and **E = 10**, what is the answer to this sum written as a letter?

   B + C – A – D = _____

10) If the code for **THEY** is **VKID**, then **YDHJ** means _____.

Score [   ] Percentage [   ] %

© 2016 Stephen Curran

3

Verbal Reasoning Test 2

1) Write the letter that will end the word in front of the brackets and start the word after the brackets. The correct letter will fit into both sets of brackets.

   FLA (____) ASH   :   SNO (____) EST

2) Write the next number in the sequence.

   110   125   140   155   170 ____

3) A four-letter word can be found at the end of one word and the beginning of the next word. Write the two words.

   Magicians often use special playing cards.   (_____ & _____)

4) Write the letters that complete the code.

   GA is to **CB** as **NJ** is to _____

5) Below are two pairs of words. One word from the list will go equally well with both pairs of words in the brackets. Underline this word.

   NEXT   HOT   WARM   BESIDE   CLOSE

   (MUGGY, HUMID)   (NEAR, ADJOINING)

6) Complete the third pair in the same way as the first two pairs. Write the new word.

   (snore, one)   (blade, ale)   (later, ____)   (_____)

7) Underline two words, one from each set of brackets, which are most opposite in meaning.

   (bury, dig, empty)   (rake, unearth, burrow)

8) Three of the five words are connected in some way. Underline the two words that do not go with these three.

   swamp   flood   bog   marsh   reed

9) Write the next letters in this sequence.

   FW HY JA LC NE _____

10) One word from the three on the left can be joined to one word from the three on the right to form a compound word. The word on the left always comes first. Underline the two words.

   (by, can, at)   (end, tack, type)

   Score [   ]   **Percentage** [   ] **%**

A B C D E F G H I J K L M N O P Q R S T U V W X Y Z

Verbal Reasoning Test 3

1) The word inside the brackets has been formed in the same way as the example given. Write the missing word.

   START (REACH) CHEER   CLEFT (_____) SHRUB

2) Write the number which will complete the sum.

   $12 \times 5 \times 2 = 59 + 33 +$ _____

3) The middle number in the last group is made in the same way as the middle numbers in the first two groups. Find the missing number. (____)

   (18 [20] 38) (19 [27] 46)
   (17 [____] 40)

4) Write the three-letter word that will complete the word in bold type.

   The girls always wanted to **PERM** on stage.   (_____)

5) Three of the four words below are given in code. The codes are not written in the same order as the words and one code is missing.

   LAKE   CALM   ROCK   SEAL

   3641   2587   1476

   Find the code for **COOLER**.   (_____)

6) Move one letter from the first word and place it into the second word to make two new words. Write the letter.

   PEDAL   WELL   (_____)

7) Underline two words, one from each set of brackets, which are most similar in meaning.

   (game, winner, result)   (loser, monopoly, outcome)

8) Complete this analogy by underlining one word from each set of brackets.

   Devil is to (horns, lived, red) as **drawer** is to (reward, chest, artist)

9) If **A = 27**, **B = 9**, **C = 15**, **D = 5** and **E = 3**, what is the answer to this sum written as a letter?

   $D \times E + C - A =$ _____

10) If the code for **DOWN** is **EPXO**, what is the code for **DUCK**?

    (_____)

Score [   ] Percentage [%]

Verbal Reasoning Test 4

1) Write the letter that will end the word in front of the brackets and start the word after the brackets. The correct letter will fit into both sets of brackets.

   SEE (____) EEP   :   LEA (____) UEL

2) Write the next number in the sequence.

   1 3 6 8 16 18 ____

3) A four-letter word can be found at the end of one word and the beginning of the next word. Write the two words.

   Mandy's biscuits were crisp and sweet.   (_____ & _____)

4) Write the letters that complete the code.

   ST is to **TX** as **UW** is to _____

5) Below are two pairs of words. One word from the list will go equally well with both pairs of words in the brackets. Underline this word.

   COMB   SEEK   FIND   UNRAVEL   ARRANGE

   (HUNT, SEARCH)   (UNTANGLE, BRUSH)

6) Complete the third pair in the same way as the first two pairs. Write the new word.

   (arena, near)   (tripe, pier)   (heart, ____)   (_____)

7) Underline two words, one from each set of brackets, which are most opposite in meaning.

   (provide, project, proceed)   (stake, stop, stifle)

8) Three of the five words are connected in some way. Underline the two words that do not go with these three.

   fix   make   attach   fasten   repair

9) Write the next letters in this sequence.

   RZ QB OD LF HH _____

10) One word from the three on the left can be joined to one word from the three on the right to form a compound word. The word on the left always comes first. Underline the two words.

   (tame, straw, fin)   (gear, dust, berry)

   Score [   ]   **Percentage** [   ] %

6

A B C D E F G H I J K L M N O P Q R S T U V W X Y Z

Verbal Reasoning Test 5

1) Complete the third pair in the same way as the first two pairs. Write the new word.

   (palace, pale)   (rotate, rate)   (belated, ____)   (_____)

2) Underline two words, one from each set of brackets, which are most opposite in meaning.

   (expect, exact, accept)   (delay, partly, refuse)

3) Three of the five words are connected in some way. Underline the two words that do not go with these three.

   tooth   hole   cavity   dentist   pit

4) Write the next letters in this sequence.

   KD HE EG BJ YN _____

5) One word from the three on the left can be joined to one word from the three on the right to form a compound word. The word on the left always comes first. Underline the two words.

   (house, flat, even)   (tend, warm, hold)

6) Write the letter that will end the word in front of the brackets and start the word after the brackets. The correct letter will fit into both sets of brackets.

   BEA (____) OWN   :   SIL (____) EAR

7) Write the next number in the sequence.

   28 28 31 27 34 26 ____

8) A four-letter word can be found at the end of one word and the beginning of the next word. Write the two words.

   The loud music kept everyone awake.   (_____ & _____)

9) Write the letters that complete the code.

   CI is to **ZF** as **GK** is to _____

10) Below are two pairs of words. One word from the list will go equally well with both pairs of words in the brackets. Underline this word.

   WASP   FASTEN   BOLT   EXIT   GRAB

   (LOCK, CATCH)   (FLEE, FLY)

   Score [   ] Percentage [%]

© 2016 Stephen Curran

7

Verbal Reasoning Test 6

1) Move one letter from the first word and place it into the second word to make two new words. Write the letter.

   SHAME   SIRE   (_____)

2) Underline two words, one from each set of brackets, which are most similar in meaning.

   (notice, sign, placard)   (spot, slip, split)

3) Complete this analogy by underlining one word from each set of brackets.

   Herd is to (heard, cattle, pasture) as **flock** is to (sheep, group, fleck)

4) If **A = 20, B = 10, C = 5, D = 50** and **E = 3**, what is the answer to this sum written as a letter?

   $D \div B \times E + C =$ _____

5) If the code for **VINE** is **ZERA**, then **TKPA** means _____.

6) The word inside the brackets has been formed in the same way as the example given. Write the missing word.

   TASTE (STEAM) MARKS   METRE (_____) SENSE

7) Write the number which will complete the sum.

   $16 + 17 + 18 = 3 \times 17 +$ _____

8) The middle number in the last group is made in the same way as the middle numbers in the first two groups. Find the missing number. (_____)

   (50 [20] 10)   (45 [15] 15)
   (48 [_____] 20)

9) Write the three-letter word that will complete the word in bold type.

   My brothers always **DIREE** over who's better at chess.   (_____)

10) Three of the four words below are given in code. The codes are not written in the same order as the words and one code is missing.

    SHIP   DESK   HIDE   CASE

    9813   4315   2743

    Find the word for the code **1574434**. (_____)

Score [   ] Percentage [   ] %

Verbal Reasoning Test 7

1) Write the letter that will end the word in front of the brackets and start the word after the brackets. The correct letter will fit into both sets of brackets.

   COR (____) ILL   :   LIN (____) NEE

2) Write the next number in the sequence.

   13 14 16 19 23 28 ____

3) A four-letter word can be found at the end of one word and the beginning of the next word. Write the two words.

   Andrew's English homework was quite messy.   (_____ & _____)

4) Write the letters that complete the code.

   EW is to **GU** as **TF** is to _____

5) Below are two pairs of words. One word from the list will go equally well with both pairs of words in the brackets. Underline this word.

   LONELY   LEAK   STRAIN   EMPTY   PLAIN

   (DESERTED, BARE)   (DRAIN, UNLOAD)

6) Complete the third pair in the same way as the first two pairs. Write the new word.

   (narrate, rant)   (damaged, made)   (pirates, ___)   (_____)

7) Underline two words, one from each set of brackets, which are most opposite in meaning.

   (testify, magnify, purify)   (reduce, reflect, remote)

8) Three of the five words are connected in some way. Underline the two words that do not go with these three.

   perfect   inferior   perform   flawless   impeccable

9) Write the next letters in this sequence.

   KH IK GN EQ CT _____

10) One word from the three on the left can be joined to one word from the three on the right to form a compound word. The word on the left always comes first. Underline the two words.

   (ours, their, your)   (elves, imps, fairies)

   Score [   ] Percentage [   ] %

Verbal Reasoning Test 8

1) Move one letter from the first word and place it into the second word to make two new words. Write the letter.

   RANGE   SORE   (_____)

2) Underline two words, one from each set of brackets, which are most similar in meaning.

   (ring, knock, call)   (sink, plug, tap)

3) Complete this analogy by underlining one word from each set of brackets.

   Mail is to (envelope, male, postman) as **pail** is to (bucket, pale, white)

4) If **A = 100, B = 5, C = 50, D = 125** and **E = 25**, what is the answer to this sum written as a letter?

   A – C + E – C = _____

5) If the code for **PLANKS** is **SJDLNQ**, what is the code for **WOODEN**?

                                                                          (_____)

6) The word inside the brackets has been formed in the same way as the example given. Write the missing word.

   DREAM (READY) DAIRY   SCARE (_____) DENTS

7) Write the number which will complete the sum.

   3 × 4 × 5 = 50 + 47 – _____

8) The middle number in the last group is made   (3 [11] 3) (4 [14] 3)
   in the same way as the middle numbers in   (4 [_____] 5)
   the first two groups. Find the missing number. (_____)

9) Write the three-letter word that will complete the word in bold type.

   Jenny and Sam wrote an **ICLE** about fashion.   (_____)

10) Three of the four words below are given in code. The codes are not written in the same order as the words and one code is missing.

    BARK   ROBE   BEAR   KITE

         8715   2697   8152

    Find the word for the code **85712**. (_____)

    Score [   ]   Percentage [   ] **%**

Verbal Reasoning Test 9

1) The word inside the brackets has been formed in the same way as the example given. Write the missing word.

   SNORE (CHEST) TEACH   METRE (_____) EARTH

2) Write the number which will complete the sum.

   $10 \times 10 \div 2 = 6 \times 7 +$ _____

3) The middle number in the last group is made in the same way as the middle numbers in the first two groups. Find the missing number. (_____)

   (23 [44] 18)   (19 [35] 13)
   (14 [_____] 15)

4) Write the three-letter word that will complete the word in bold type.

   You will improve if you **PRICE** every day.   (_____)

5) Three of the four words below are given in code. The codes are not written in the same order as the words and one code is missing.

   FISH   PEAS   CHIP   SHOP

   8461   7491   1257

   Find the code for **SPACE**.   (_____)

6) Move one letter from the first word and place it into the second word to make two new words. Write the letter.

   SPLIT   GROW   (_____)

7) Underline two words, one from each set of brackets, which are most similar in meaning.

   (pledge, plead, question)   (respond, promise, require)

8) Complete this analogy by underlining one word from each set of brackets.

   Spoke is to (wheel, bicycle, speak) as **laid** is to (lay, down, egg)

9) If **A = 24, B = 36, C = 3, D = 8** and **E = 2**, what is the answer to this sum written as a letter?

   $B \div E + C + C =$ _____

10) If the code for **BEGAN** is **YBDXK**, what is the code for **AWFUL**?

    (_____)

Score [   ]   Percentage [   ] **%**

Verbal Reasoning Test 10

1) Write the letter that will end the word in front of the brackets and start the word after the brackets. The correct letter will fit into both sets of brackets.

   DUN (____) NAW   :   LON (____) ATE

2) Write the next number in the sequence.

   1 2 3 5 8 13 _____

3) A four-letter word can be found at the end of one word and the beginning of the next word. Write the two words.

   Thick snow covered those mountain tops.   (_____ & _____)

4) Write the letters that complete the code.

   GQ is to **ER** as **QG** is to _____

5) Below are two pairs of words. One word from the list will go equally well with both pairs of words in the brackets. Underline this word.

   FIX   RECTIFY   NAIL   SORT   RESTORE

   (ATTACH, STICK)   (MEND, REPAIR)

6) Complete the third pair in the same way as the first two pairs. Write the new word.

   (flake, flame)   (crate, crave)   (stare, ____)   (_____)

7) Underline two words, one from each set of brackets, which are most opposite in meaning.

   (hesitant, ignorant, certain)   (direct, decisive, defiant)

8) Three of the five words are connected in some way. Underline the two words that do not go with these three.

   sweet   rich   prosperous   dessert   wealthy

9) Write the next letters in this sequence.

   GF FI EL DO CR _____

10) One word from the three on the left can be joined to one word from the three on the right to form a compound word. The word on the left always comes first. Underline the two words.

   (rode, way, lane)   (word, ward, work)

Score ☐   Percentage ☐ %

Verbal Reasoning Test 11

1) The word inside the brackets has been formed in the same way as the example given. Write the missing word.

   CLOTH (CATCH) ACTOR   FRIED (_____) INLET

2) Write the number which will complete the sum.

   $48 \div 2 \div 3 = 30 - 17 -$ _____

3) The middle number in the last group is made in the same way as the middle numbers in the first two groups. Find the missing number. (_____)

   (16 [22] 5)   (18 [16] 10)
   (30 [____] 14)

4) Write the three-letter word that will complete the word in bold type.

   There is a **GER** in the sett over there.   (_____)

5) Three of the four words below are given in code. The codes are not written in the same order as the words and one code is missing.

   KITE   BEAR   ROBE   BARK

        2697   8715   8152

   Find the code for **BEATER**.   (_____)

6) Move one letter from the first word and place it into the second word to make two new words. Write the letter.

   BLEND   SAKE   (_____)

7) Underline two words, one from each set of brackets, which are most similar in meaning.

   (tumble, mount, peak)   (clench, valley, climb)

8) Complete this analogy by underlining one word from each set of brackets.

   Doctor is to (nurse, practise, hospital) as **teacher** is to
   (pupil, professor, school)

9) If **A = 2**, **B = 10**, **C = 3**, **D = 15** and **E = 5**, what is the answer to this sum written as a letter?

   $B \times D \div E \div B =$ _____

10) If the code for **POEM** is **TSIQ**, then **WSRK** means _____.

Score [   ]   Percentage [   ] %

13

Verbal Reasoning Test 12

1) Write the letter that will end the word in front of the brackets and start the word after the brackets. The correct letter will fit into both sets of brackets.

   GRI (____) ALE   :   SLA (____) ANT

2) Write the next number in the sequence.

   3 4 7 11 18 29 _____

3) A four-letter word can be found at the end of one word and the beginning of the next word. Write the two words.

   The sailor drifted across the ocean.   (_____ & _____)

4) Write the letters that complete the code.

   IV is to **MU** as **LQ** is to _____

5) Below are two pairs of words. One word from the list will go equally well with both pairs of words in the brackets. Underline this word.

   SINK   TROUBLED   TORMENT   UPSET   DROOP

   (TOPPLE, CAPSIZE)   (DISTRESSED, DISTURBED)

6) Complete the third pair in the same way as the first two pairs. Write the new word.

   (regret, greet)   (pastel, steal)   (metals, ____)   (_____)

7) Underline two words, one from each set of brackets, which are most opposite in meaning.

   (clumsy, lenient, erratic)   (awkward, severe, honest)

8) Three of the five words are connected in some way. Underline the two words that do not go with these three.

   diamond   silver   gold   ruby   emerald

9) Write the next letters in this sequence.

   DF AG XI UJ RL _____

10) One word from the three on the left can be joined to one word from the three on the right to form a compound word. The word on the left always comes first. Underline the two words.

    (per, over, run)   (face, chase, fume)

    Score [   ]   **Percentage** [   ] **%**

A B C D E F G H I J K L M N O P Q R S T U V W X Y Z

Verbal Reasoning Test 13

1) Complete the third pair in the same way as the first two pairs. Write the new word.

   (disused, side)   (divider, dire)   (caskets, ____)   (_____)

2) Underline two words, one from each set of brackets, which are most opposite in meaning.

   (ready, steady, charge)   (unstable, fixed, faulty)

3) Three of the five words are connected in some way. Underline the two words that do not go with these three.

   melt   boil   defrost   heat   thaw

4) Write the next letters in this sequence.

   EU AQ DT ZP CS _____

5) One word from the three on the left can be joined to one word from the three on the right to form a compound word. The word on the left always comes first. Underline the two words.

   (break, snap, cut)   (though, through, tough)

6) Write the letter that will end the word in front of the brackets and start the word after the brackets. The correct letter will fit into both sets of brackets.

   BUR (___) EAR   :   FLO (___) IER

7) Write the next number in the sequence.

   275 265 245 215 175 _____

8) A four-letter word can be found at the end of one word and the beginning of the next word. Write the two words.

   Keep calm when the alarm rings.   (_____ & _____)

9) Write the letters that complete the code.

   GB is to **DZ** as **NK** is to _____

10) Below are two pairs of words. One word from the list will go equally well with both pairs of words in the brackets. Underline this word.

   ATTACHED   SPRING   SKIP   BONDED   BOUND

   (LEAP, JUMP)   (TIED, TETHERED)

   Score [   ] Percentage [%]

Verbal Reasoning Test 14

1) Move one letter from the first word and place it into the second word to make two new words. Write the letter.

   LANCE   AREA (_____)

2) Underline two words, one from each set of brackets, which are most similar in meaning.

   (mystery, confess, mimic)   (confuse, puzzle, mystify)

3) Complete this analogy by underlining one word from each set of brackets.

   Cease is to (crease, grab, start) as **cheap** is to (dear, heap, bird)

4) If **A = 3, B = 7, C = 12, D = 4** and **E = 15**, what is the answer to this sum written as a letter?

   $D \times E \div C + B =$ _____

5) If the code for **VERMIN** is **BZVJKM**, what is the code for **OCEANS**?

   (_____)

6) The word inside the brackets has been formed in the same way as the example given. Write the missing word.

   LIMIT (MILES) BLESS   DISCO (_____) CARED

7) Write the number which will complete the sum.

   $81 \div 9 - 2 = 40 \div 2 -$ _____

8) The middle number in the last group is made in the same way as the middle numbers in the first two groups. Find the missing number. **(17 [30] 18)   (26 [49] 28)**
   (14 [____] 36)
   (_____)

9) Write the three-letter word that will complete the word in bold type.

   The skater **GED** gracefully across the ice. (_____)

10) Three of the four words below are given in code. The codes are not written in the same order as the words and one code is missing.

    THEM   ZERO   MARE   HAZE

    5314   4281   6187

    Find the word for the code **475318**.

    (_____)

Score [   ] Percentage [   ] %

Verbal Reasoning Test 15

1) Write the letter that will end the word in front of the brackets and start the word after the brackets. The correct letter will fit into both sets of brackets.

   DEA (____) AST   :   MAI (____) ATE

2) Write the next number in the sequence.

   12 15 19 22 26 29 _____

3) A four-letter word can be found at the end of one word and the beginning of the next word. Write the two words.

   Some genies live inside old lamps.   (_____ & _____)

4) Write the letters that complete the code.

   CH is to **EJ** as **EJ** is to _____

5) Below are two pairs of words. One word from the list will go equally well with both pairs of words in the brackets. Underline this word.

   STRIP   FIGHT   STRING   ROW   QUEUE

   (ARGUE, QUARREL)   (LINE, COLUMN)

6) Complete the third pair in the same way as the first two pairs. Write the new word.

   (least, mast)   (shank, tank)   (blame, ___)   (_____)

7) Underline two words, one from each set of brackets, which are most opposite in meaning.

   (bright, occupy, seldom)   (often, rare, quietly)

8) Three of the five words are connected in some way. Underline the two words that do not go with these three.

   begin   end   start   finish   conclude

9) Write the next letters in this sequence.

   JK KM LO MQ NS _____

10) One word from the three on the left can be joined to one word from the three on the right to form a compound word. The word on the left always comes first. Underline the two words.

   (short, rum, flow)   (wing, age, here)

Score [   ]   Percentage [   ] %

Verbal Reasoning Test 16

1) Move one letter from the first word and place it into the second word to make two new words. Write the letter.

   HEART   MOOR   (_____)

2) Underline two words, one from each set of brackets, which are most similar in meaning.

   (remind, remove, remedy)   (placed, cure, behind)

3) Complete this analogy by underlining one word from each set of brackets.

   Pick is to (mix, choose, shovel) as **move** is to (shift, house, motivate)

4) If $A = 4$, $B = 11$, $C = 7$, $D = 21$ and $E = 3$, what is the answer to this sum written as a letter?

   $C \times E - D + A =$ _____

5) If the code for **SHAFT** is **PIXGQ**, then **JJKFO** means _____.

6) The word inside the brackets has been formed in the same way as the example given. Write the missing word.

   BLAME (CABLE) CLEAN   ADORE (_____) TEARS

7) Write the number which will complete the sum.

   $16 + 15 + 14 = 13 + 17 +$ _____

8) The middle number in the last group is made in the same way as the middle numbers in the first two groups. Find the missing number.   **(9 [60] 7)   (8 [77] 10)   (6 [_____] 9)**   (_____)

9) Write the three-letter word that will complete the word in bold type.

   The waiter looked like a **GUIN** in his black suit.   (_____)

10) Three of the four words below are given in code. The codes are not written in the same order as the words and one code is missing.

   CARE   SOCK   RENT   ROSE

   9865   6874   7395

   Find the word for the code **795365**.

   (_____)

   Score [   ]   Percentage [%]

Verbal Reasoning Test 17

1) The word inside the brackets has been formed in the same way as the example given. Write the missing word.

   TOAST (SHOUT) SOUTH   BAILS (_____) LADLE

2) Write the number which will complete the sum.

   $106 - 19 - 21 = 2 \times 3 \times$ _____

3) The middle number in the last group is made in the same way as the middle numbers in the first two groups. Find the missing number. (_____)   (7 [9] 25) (18 [11] 40) (16 [____] 36)

4) Write the three-letter word that will complete the word in bold type.

   The pictures hung around the walls of the **GERY**.   (_____)

5) Three of the four words below are given in code. The codes are not written in the same order as the words and one code is missing.

   WASH   BEAT   DAWB   SHED

   8254   3782   9571

   Find the code for **BASHED**.   (_____)

6) Move one letter from the first word and place it into the second word to make two new words. Write the letter.

   CLAMP   PATH   (____)

7) Underline two words, one from each set of brackets, which are most similar in meaning.

   (divide, subtract, multiply)   (attach, attract, split)

8) Complete this analogy by underlining one word from each set of brackets.

   Duck is to (drake, avoid, pond) as **hen** is to (chicken, cockerel, egg)

9) If **A = 5, B = 10, C = 2, D = 15** and **E = 7**, what is the answer to this sum written as a letter?

   $B \times E \div A - E =$ _____

10) If the code for **MILE** is **IKHG**, then **LQOV** means _____.

Score [   ]   Percentage [   ] %

ABCDEFGHIJKLMNOPQRSTUVWXYZ

Verbal Reasoning Test 18

1) Write the letter that will end the word in front of the brackets and start the word after the brackets. The correct letter will fit into both sets of brackets.

   PAI (____) AIL   :   STA (____) OCK

2) Write the next number in the sequence.

   2 15 3 14 5 12 8 ____

3) A four-letter word can be found at the end of one word and the beginning of the next word. Write the two words.

   Claire's piano teacher was very pleased.   (_____ & _____)

4) Write the letters that complete the code.

   SL is to **PN** as **RG** is to _____

5) Below are two pairs of words. One word from the list will go equally well with both pairs of words in the brackets. Underline this word.

   QUICK   PROMPT   EXPRESS   CHAT   CONVERSE
   (SPEAK, STATE)   (FAST, RAPID)

6) Complete the third pair in the same way as the first two pairs. Write the new word.

   (remove, ever)   (danger, read)   (sachet, _____)   (_____)

7) Underline two words, one from each set of brackets, which are most opposite in meaning.

   (imitate, start, illegal)   (begin, benign, lawful)

8) Three of the five words are connected in some way. Underline the two words that do not go with these three.

   misplace   mislead   lose   fool   mislay

9) Write the next letters in this sequence.

   CD EE GG IJ KN _____

10) One word from the three on the left can be joined to one word from the three on the right to form a compound word. The word on the left always comes first. Underline the two words.

   (smile, mouth, grin)   (part, full, piece)

Score [   ] Percentage [   ] %

20   © 2016 Stephen Curran

Verbal Reasoning Test 19

1) The word inside the brackets has been formed in the same way as the example given. Write the missing word.

LEAST (SLIME) TIMES   HORSE (_____) HOVER

2) Write the number which will complete the sum.

103 – 25 – 28 = 14 + 16 + _____

3) The middle number in the last group is made in the same way as the middle numbers in the first two groups. Find the missing number. (____)

(6 [19] 7) (9 [29] 11)
(11 [____] 9)

4) Write the three-letter word that will complete the word in bold type.

Sally and her friends go to **BRIES** on a Friday.   (_____)

5) Three of the four words below are given in code. The codes are not written in the same order as the words and one code is missing.

SNUG   NEWT   PENS   PUNT

3479   1742   4862

Find the code for **WEEPS**.   (_____)

6) Move one letter from the first word and place it into the second word to make two new words. Write the letter.

WEARY   CLAN   (_____)

7) Underline two words, one from each set of brackets, which are most similar in meaning.

(disperse, converge, require)   (scatter, hesitate, enforce)

8) Complete this analogy by underlining one word from each set of brackets.

Mane is to (lion, main, chief) as **paws** is to (swap, cease, pause)

9) If **A = 100, B = 25, C = 5, D = 50** and **E = 10**, what is the answer to this sum written as a letter?

$A \div E + C + E =$ ____

10) If the code for **PACK** is **QYFG**, then **CCDN** means _____.

Score [   ] Percentage [   ] %

Verbal Reasoning Test 20

1) Write the letter that will end the word in front of the brackets and start the word after the brackets. The correct letter will fit into both sets of brackets.

   SLU (____) USH   :   SIN (____) OAL

2) Write the next number in the sequence.

   19 24 28 33 37 42 ____

3) A four-letter word can be found at the end of one word and the beginning of the next word. Write the two words.

   The baker baked bread and cakes.   (_____ & _____)

4) Write the letters that complete the code.

   HS is to **GQ** as **RI** is to _____

5) Below are two pairs of words. One word from the list will go equally well with both pairs of words in the brackets. Underline this word.

   MAKE   MOULD   CARVE   MILDEW   ROT

   (FUNGUS, GROWTH)   (SHAPE, SCULPT)

6) Complete the third pair in the same way as the first two pairs. Write the new word.

   (railway, wail)   (develop, love)   (charter, ____)   (_____)

7) Underline two words, one from each set of brackets, which are most opposite in meaning.

   (destroy, deter, dismiss)   (disobey, create, linger)

8) Three of the five words are connected in some way. Underline the two words that do not go with these three.

   tie   scarf   bind   close   tether

9) Write the next letters in this sequence.

   FH HJ JL LN NP _____

10) One word from the three on the left can be joined to one word from the three on the right to form a compound word. The word on the left always comes first. Underline the two words.

    (gasp, puff, blow)   (wing, in, red)

    Score [   ]   Percentage [%]

Multiple-choice Answer Sheet
11+ Verbal Reasoning Year 5-7 GL & Other Styles Testbook 5

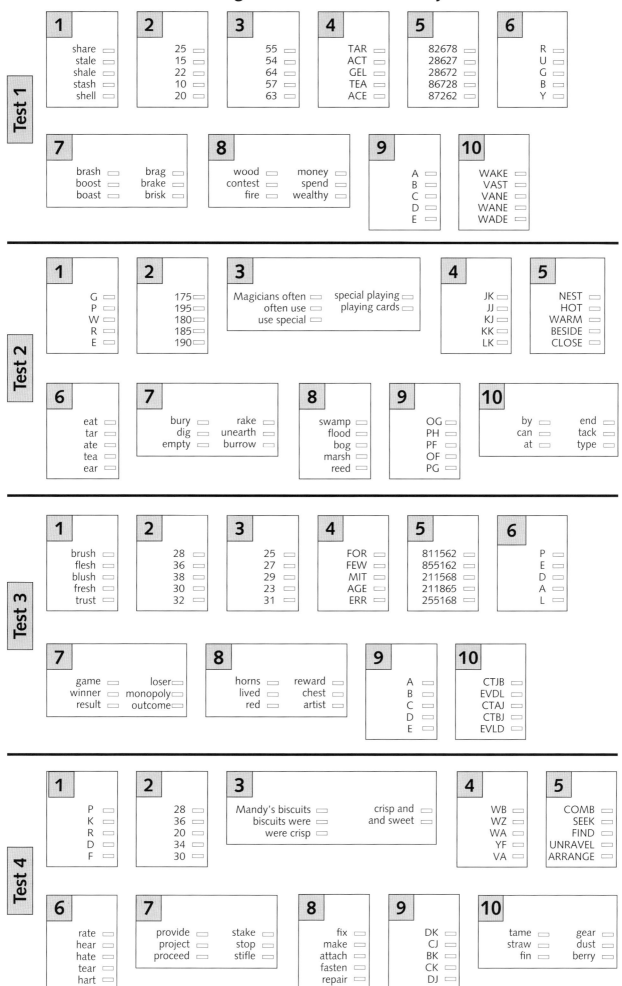

Test 1

1
- share
- stale
- shale
- stash
- shell

2
- 25
- 15
- 22
- 10
- 20

3
- 55
- 54
- 64
- 57
- 63

4
- TAR
- ACT
- GEL
- TEA
- ACE

5
- 82678
- 28627
- 28672
- 86728
- 87262

6
- R
- U
- G
- B
- Y

7
- brash
- boost
- boast
- brag
- brake
- brisk

8
- wood
- contest
- fire
- money
- spend
- wealthy

9
- A
- B
- C
- D
- E

10
- WAKE
- VAST
- VANE
- WANE
- WADE

Test 2

1
- G
- P
- W
- R
- E

2
- 175
- 195
- 180
- 185
- 190

3
- Magicians often
- often use
- use special
- special playing
- playing cards

4
- JK
- JJ
- KJ
- KK
- LK

5
- NEST
- HOT
- WARM
- BESIDE
- CLOSE

6
- eat
- tar
- ate
- tea
- ear

7
- bury
- dig
- empty
- rake
- unearth
- burrow

8
- swamp
- flood
- bog
- marsh
- reed

9
- OG
- PH
- PF
- OF
- PG

10
- by
- can
- at
- end
- tack
- type

Test 3

1
- brush
- flesh
- blush
- fresh
- trust

2
- 28
- 36
- 38
- 30
- 32

3
- 25
- 27
- 29
- 23
- 31

4
- FOR
- FEW
- MIT
- AGE
- ERR

5
- 811562
- 855162
- 211568
- 211865
- 255168

6
- P
- E
- D
- A
- L

7
- game
- winner
- result
- loser
- monopoly
- outcome

8
- horns
- lived
- red
- reward
- chest
- artist

9
- A
- B
- C
- D
- E

10
- CTJB
- EVDL
- CTAJ
- CTBJ
- EVLD

Test 4

1
- P
- K
- R
- D
- F

2
- 28
- 36
- 20
- 34
- 30

3
- Mandy's biscuits
- biscuits were
- were crisp
- crisp and
- and sweet

4
- WB
- WZ
- WA
- YF
- VA

5
- COMB
- SEEK
- FIND
- UNRAVEL
- ARRANGE

6
- rate
- hear
- hate
- tear
- hart

7
- provide
- project
- proceed
- stake
- stop
- stifle

8
- fix
- make
- attach
- fasten
- repair

9
- DK
- CJ
- BK
- CK
- DJ

10
- tame
- straw
- fin
- gear
- dust
- berry

Multiple-choice Answer Sheet
11+ Verbal Reasoning Year 5-7 GL & Other Styles Testbook 5

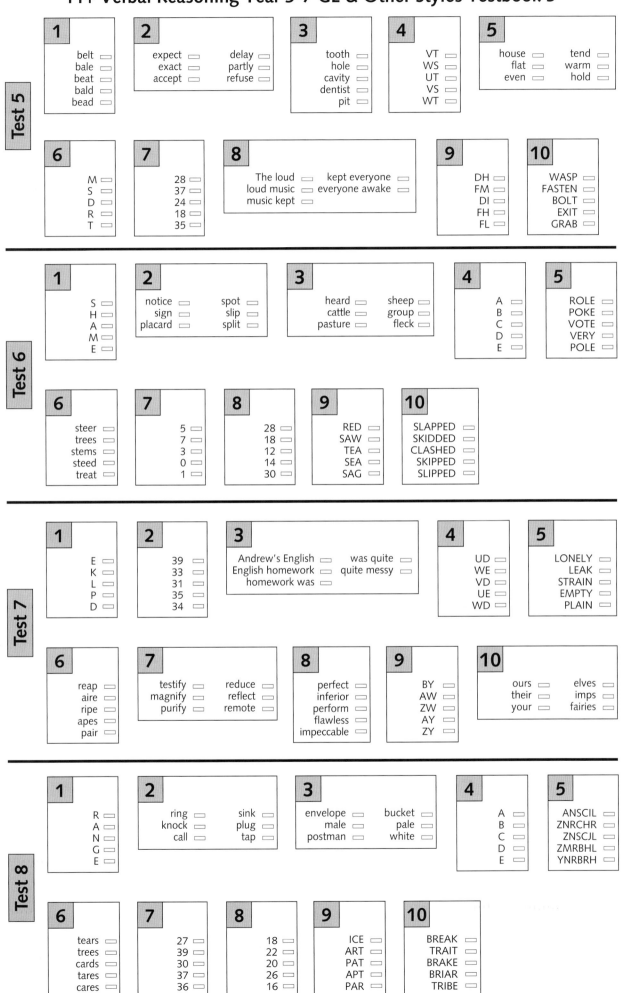

Test 5

1
- belt
- bale
- beat
- bald
- bead

2
- expect
- exact
- accept
- delay
- partly
- refuse

3
- tooth
- hole
- cavity
- dentist
- pit

4
- VT
- WS
- UT
- VS
- WT

5
- house
- flat
- even
- tend
- warm
- hold

6
- M
- S
- D
- R
- T

7
- 28
- 37
- 24
- 18
- 35

8
- The loud
- loud music
- music kept
- kept everyone
- everyone awake

9
- DH
- FM
- DI
- FH
- FL

10
- WASP
- FASTEN
- BOLT
- EXIT
- GRAB

Test 6

1
- S
- H
- A
- M
- E

2
- notice
- sign
- placard
- spot
- slip
- split

3
- heard
- cattle
- pasture
- sheep
- group
- fleck

4
- A
- B
- C
- D
- E

5
- ROLE
- POKE
- VOTE
- VERY
- POLE

6
- steer
- trees
- stems
- steed
- treat

7
- 5
- 7
- 3
- 0
- 1

8
- 28
- 18
- 12
- 14
- 30

9
- RED
- SAW
- TEA
- SEA
- SAG

10
- SLAPPED
- SKIDDED
- CLASHED
- SKIPPED
- SLIPPED

Test 7

1
- E
- K
- L
- P
- D

2
- 39
- 33
- 31
- 35
- 34

3
- Andrew's English
- English homework
- homework was
- was quite
- quite messy

4
- UD
- WE
- VD
- UE
- WD

5
- LONELY
- LEAK
- STRAIN
- EMPTY
- PLAIN

6
- reap
- aire
- ripe
- apes
- pair

7
- testify
- magnify
- purify
- reduce
- reflect
- remote

8
- perfect
- inferior
- perform
- flawless
- impeccable

9
- BY
- AW
- ZW
- AY
- ZY

10
- ours
- their
- your
- elves
- imps
- fairies

Test 8

1
- R
- A
- N
- G
- E

2
- ring
- knock
- call
- sink
- plug
- tap

3
- envelope
- male
- postman
- bucket
- pale
- white

4
- A
- B
- C
- D
- E

5
- ANSCIL
- ZNRCHR
- ZNSCJL
- ZMRBHL
- YNRBRH

6
- tears
- trees
- cards
- tares
- cares

7
- 27
- 39
- 30
- 37
- 36

8
- 18
- 22
- 20
- 26
- 16

9
- ICE
- ART
- PAT
- APT
- PAR

10
- BREAK
- TRAIT
- BRAKE
- BRIAR
- TRIBE

Multiple-choice Answer Sheet
11+ Verbal Reasoning Year 5-7 GL & Other Styles Testbook 5

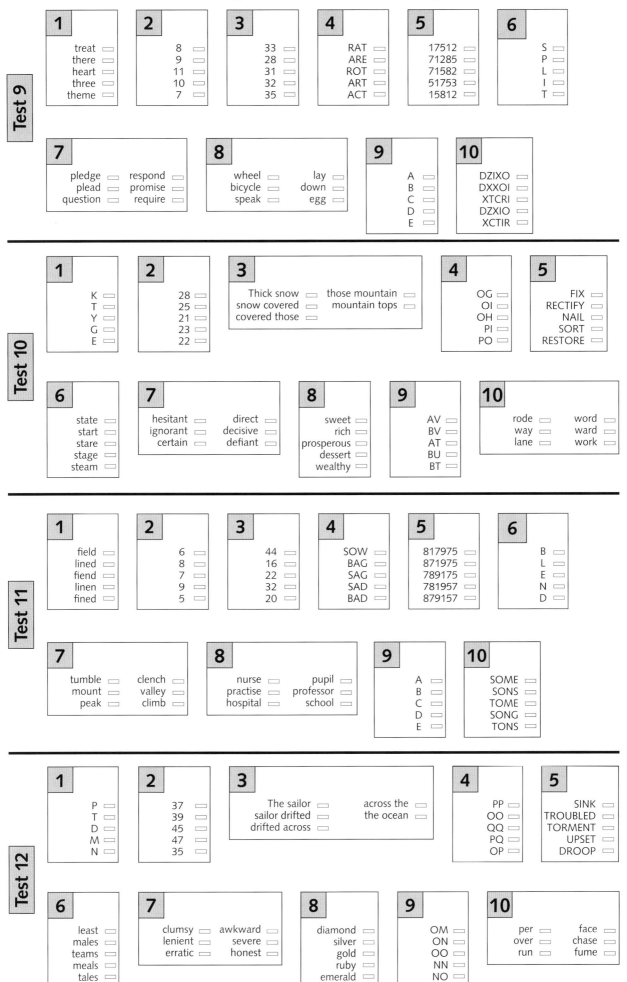

Test 9

1
- treat ▭
- there ▭
- heart ▭
- three ▭
- theme ▭

2
- 8 ▭
- 9 ▭
- 11 ▭
- 10 ▭
- 7 ▭

3
- 33 ▭
- 28 ▭
- 31 ▭
- 32 ▭
- 35 ▭

4
- RAT ▭
- ARE ▭
- ROT ▭
- ART ▭
- ACT ▭

5
- 17512 ▭
- 71285 ▭
- 71582 ▭
- 51753 ▭
- 15812 ▭

6
- S ▭
- P ▭
- L ▭
- I ▭
- T ▭

7
- pledge ▭
- plead ▭
- question ▭
- respond ▭
- promise ▭
- require ▭

8
- wheel ▭
- bicycle ▭
- speak ▭
- lay ▭
- down ▭
- egg ▭

9
- A ▭
- B ▭
- C ▭
- D ▭
- E ▭

10
- DZIXO ▭
- DXXOI ▭
- XTCRI ▭
- DZXIO ▭
- XCTIR ▭

Test 10

1
- K ▭
- T ▭
- Y ▭
- G ▭
- E ▭

2
- 28 ▭
- 25 ▭
- 21 ▭
- 23 ▭
- 22 ▭

3
- Thick snow ▭
- snow covered ▭
- covered those ▭
- those mountain ▭
- mountain tops ▭

4
- OG ▭
- OI ▭
- OH ▭
- PI ▭
- PO ▭

5
- FIX ▭
- RECTIFY ▭
- NAIL ▭
- SORT ▭
- RESTORE ▭

6
- state ▭
- start ▭
- stare ▭
- stage ▭
- steam ▭

7
- hesitant ▭
- ignorant ▭
- certain ▭
- direct ▭
- decisive ▭
- defiant ▭

8
- sweet ▭
- rich ▭
- prosperous ▭
- dessert ▭
- wealthy ▭

9
- AV ▭
- BV ▭
- AT ▭
- BU ▭
- BT ▭

10
- rode ▭
- way ▭
- lane ▭
- word ▭
- ward ▭
- work ▭

Test 11

1
- field ▭
- lined ▭
- fiend ▭
- linen ▭
- fined ▭

2
- 6 ▭
- 8 ▭
- 7 ▭
- 9 ▭
- 5 ▭

3
- 44 ▭
- 16 ▭
- 22 ▭
- 32 ▭
- 20 ▭

4
- SOW ▭
- BAG ▭
- SAG ▭
- SAD ▭
- BAD ▭

5
- 817975 ▭
- 871975 ▭
- 789175 ▭
- 781957 ▭
- 879157 ▭

6
- B ▭
- L ▭
- E ▭
- N ▭
- D ▭

7
- tumble ▭
- mount ▭
- peak ▭
- clench ▭
- valley ▭
- climb ▭

8
- nurse ▭
- practise ▭
- hospital ▭
- pupil ▭
- professor ▭
- school ▭

9
- A ▭
- B ▭
- C ▭
- D ▭
- E ▭

10
- SOME ▭
- SONS ▭
- TOME ▭
- SONG ▭
- TONS ▭

Test 12

1
- P ▭
- T ▭
- D ▭
- M ▭
- N ▭

2
- 37 ▭
- 39 ▭
- 45 ▭
- 47 ▭
- 35 ▭

3
- The sailor ▭
- sailor drifted ▭
- drifted across ▭
- across the ▭
- the ocean ▭

4
- PP ▭
- OO ▭
- QQ ▭
- PQ ▭
- OP ▭

5
- SINK ▭
- TROUBLED ▭
- TORMENT ▭
- UPSET ▭
- DROOP ▭

6
- least ▭
- males ▭
- teams ▭
- meals ▭
- tales ▭

7
- clumsy ▭
- lenient ▭
- erratic ▭
- awkward ▭
- severe ▭
- honest ▭

8
- diamond ▭
- silver ▭
- gold ▭
- ruby ▭
- emerald ▭

9
- OM ▭
- ON ▭
- OO ▭
- NN ▭
- NO ▭

10
- per ▭
- over ▭
- run ▭
- face ▭
- chase ▭
- fume ▭

Multiple-choice Answer Sheet
11+ Verbal Reasoning Year 5-7 GL & Other Styles Testbook 5

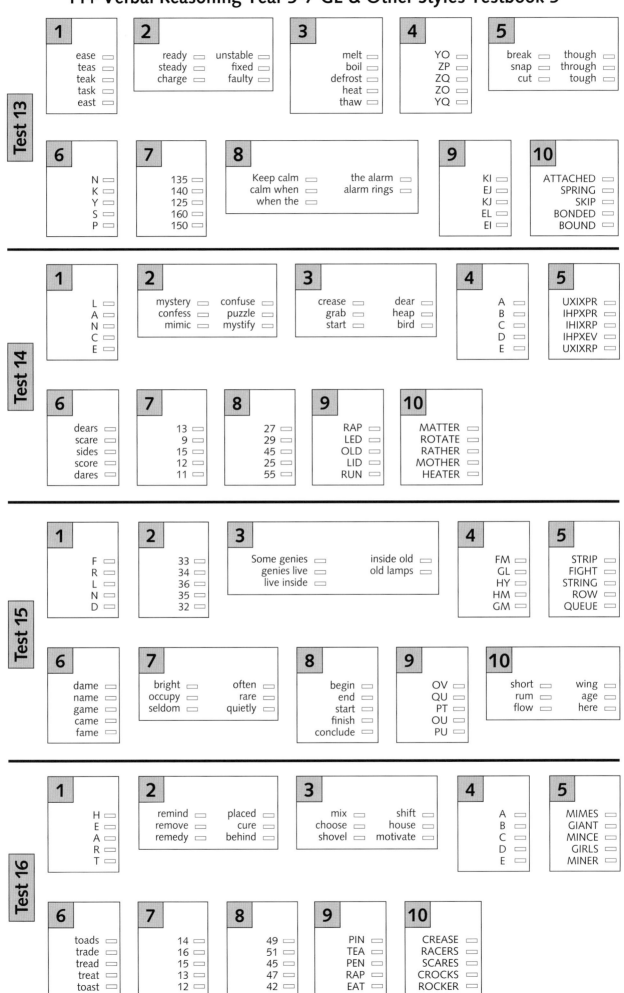

Test 13

1
- ease
- teas
- teak
- task
- east

2
- ready / unstable
- steady / fixed
- charge / faulty

3
- melt
- boil
- defrost
- heat
- thaw

4
- YO
- ZP
- ZQ
- ZO
- YQ

5
- break / though
- snap / through
- cut / tough

6
- N
- K
- Y
- S
- P

7
- 135
- 140
- 125
- 160
- 150

8
- Keep calm / the alarm
- calm when / alarm rings
- when the

9
- KI
- EJ
- KJ
- EL
- EI

10
- ATTACHED
- SPRING
- SKIP
- BONDED
- BOUND

Test 14

1
- L
- A
- N
- C
- E

2
- mystery / confuse
- confess / puzzle
- mimic / mystify

3
- crease / dear
- grab / heap
- start / bird

4
- A
- B
- C
- D
- E

5
- UXIXPR
- IHPXPR
- IHIXRP
- IHPXEV
- UXIXRP

6
- dears
- scare
- sides
- score
- dares

7
- 13
- 9
- 15
- 12
- 11

8
- 27
- 29
- 45
- 25
- 55

9
- RAP
- LED
- OLD
- LID
- RUN

10
- MATTER
- ROTATE
- RATHER
- MOTHER
- HEATER

Test 15

1
- F
- R
- L
- N
- D

2
- 33
- 34
- 36
- 35
- 32

3
- Some genies / inside old
- genies live / old lamps
- live inside

4
- FM
- GL
- HY
- HM
- GM

5
- STRIP
- FIGHT
- STRING
- ROW
- QUEUE

6
- dame
- name
- game
- came
- fame

7
- bright / often
- occupy / rare
- seldom / quietly

8
- begin
- end
- start
- finish
- conclude

9
- OV
- QU
- PT
- OU
- PU

10
- short / wing
- rum / age
- flow / here

Test 16

1
- H
- E
- A
- R
- T

2
- remind / placed
- remove / cure
- remedy / behind

3
- mix / shift
- choose / house
- shovel / motivate

4
- A
- B
- C
- D
- E

5
- MIMES
- GIANT
- MINCE
- GIRLS
- MINER

6
- toads
- trade
- tread
- treat
- toast

7
- 14
- 16
- 15
- 13
- 12

8
- 49
- 51
- 45
- 47
- 42

9
- PIN
- TEA
- PEN
- RAP
- EAT

10
- CREASE
- RACERS
- SCARES
- CROCKS
- ROCKER

Multiple-choice Answer Sheet
11+ Verbal Reasoning Year 5-7 GL & Other Styles Testbook 5

Test 17

1
- label ☐
- leads ☐
- bales ☐
- loads ☐
- beads ☐

2
- 7 ☐
- 13 ☐
- 9 ☐
- 11 ☐
- 8 ☐

3
- 25 ☐
- 10 ☐
- 20 ☐
- 27 ☐
- 16 ☐

4
- ALL ☐
- RED ☐
- MAT ☐
- HUT ☐
- PUT ☐

5
- 657245 ☐
- 987542 ☐
- 618547 ☐
- 978254 ☐
- 675245 ☐

6
- C ☐
- L ☐
- A ☐
- M ☐
- P ☐

7
- divide ☐
- subtract ☐
- multiply ☐
- attach ☐
- attract ☐
- split ☐

8
- drake ☐
- avoid ☐
- pond ☐
- chicken ☐
- cockerel ☐
- egg ☐

9
- A ☐
- B ☐
- C ☐
- D ☐
- E ☐

10
- HAMS ☐
- PAST ☐
- POSE ☐
- HOLE ☐
- POST ☐

Test 18

1
- D ☐
- R ☐
- N ☐
- L ☐
- W ☐

2
- 10 ☐
- 11 ☐
- 12 ☐
- 9 ☐
- 8 ☐

3
- Claire's piano ☐
- piano teacher ☐
- teacher was ☐
- was very ☐
- very pleased ☐

4
- OI ☐
- UJ ☐
- OJ ☐
- UE ☐
- UI ☐

5
- QUICK ☐
- PROMPT ☐
- EXPRESS ☐
- CHAT ☐
- CONVERSE ☐

6
- teas ☐
- seat ☐
- chat ☐
- each ☐
- heat ☐

7
- imitate ☐
- start ☐
- illegal ☐
- begin ☐
- benign ☐
- lawful ☐

8
- misplace ☐
- mislead ☐
- lose ☐
- fool ☐
- mislay ☐

9
- NS ☐
- MT ☐
- MR ☐
- MS ☐
- NT ☐

10
- smile ☐
- mouth ☐
- grin ☐
- part ☐
- full ☐
- piece ☐

Test 19

1
- shoes ☐
- verse ☐
- sheer ☐
- rover ☐
- shove ☐

2
- 21 ☐
- 23 ☐
- 20 ☐
- 25 ☐
- 29 ☐

3
- 31 ☐
- 29 ☐
- 25 ☐
- 20 ☐
- 40 ☐

4
- ROW ☐
- ORE ☐
- RAP ☐
- ART ☐
- OWN ☐

5
- 67714 ☐
- 57723 ☐
- 68813 ☐
- 57714 ☐
- 58814 ☐

6
- W ☐
- E ☐
- A ☐
- R ☐
- Y ☐

7
- disperse ☐
- converge ☐
- require ☐
- scatter ☐
- hesitate ☐
- enforce ☐

8
- lion ☐
- main ☐
- chief ☐
- swap ☐
- cease ☐
- pause ☐

9
- A ☐
- B ☐
- C ☐
- D ☐
- E ☐

10
- BEET ☐
- BEAD ☐
- BEAT ☐
- BEAR ☐
- BEER ☐

Test 20

1
- M ☐
- G ☐
- R ☐
- S ☐
- D ☐

2
- 45 ☐
- 44 ☐
- 46 ☐
- 48 ☐
- 47 ☐

3
- The baker ☐
- baker baked ☐
- baked bread ☐
- bread and ☐
- and cakes ☐

4
- RH ☐
- QG ☐
- PI ☐
- PG ☐
- QH ☐

5
- MAKE ☐
- MOULD ☐
- CARVE ☐
- MILDEW ☐
- ROT ☐

6
- tare ☐
- tear ☐
- rate ☐
- arch ☐
- each ☐

7
- destroy ☐
- deter ☐
- dismiss ☐
- disobey ☐
- create ☐
- linger ☐

8
- tie ☐
- scarf ☐
- bind ☐
- close ☐
- tether ☐

9
- PR ☐
- PS ☐
- PT ☐
- OR ☐
- OS ☐

10
- gasp ☐
- puff ☐
- blow ☐
- wing ☐
- in ☐
- red ☐

Answers

Test 1
1) SHALE
2) 20
3) 64
4) ACT
5) 82678
6) G
7) boast & brag
8) contest & wealthy
9) B
10) WADE

Test 2
1) W
2) 185
3) Magicians & often (soft)
4) JK
5) CLOSE
6) tar
7) bury & unearth
8) flood & reed
9) PG
10) at & tack

Test 3
1) fresh
2) 28
3) 23
4) FOR
5) 855162
6) D
7) result & outcome
8) lived & reward
9) E
10) EVDL

Test 4
1) D
2) 36

3) crisp & and (span)
4) VA
5) COMB
6) RATE
7) proceed & stop
8) make & repair
9) CJ
10) straw & berry

Test 5
1) bald
2) accept & refuse
3) tooth & dentist
4) VS
5) house & hold
6) T
7) 37
8) music & kept (sick)
9) DH
10) BOLT

Test 6
1) H
2) notice & spot
3) cattle & sheep
4) A
5) POLE
6) trees
7) 0
8) 14
9) SAG
10) SKIDDED

Test 7
1) K
2) 34
3) quite & messy (item)
4) VD
5) EMPTY
6) ripe

7) magnify & reduce
8) inferior & perform
9) AW
10) ours & elves

Test 8
1) N
2) knock & tap
3) male & pale
4) E
5) ZMRBHL
6) cards
7) 37
8) 22
9) ART
10) BREAK

Test 9
1) theme
2) 8
3) 32
4) ACT
5) 71582
6) L
7) pledge & promise
8) speak & lay
9) A
10) XTCRI

Test 10
1) G
2) 21
3) mountain & tops (into)
4) OH
5) FIX
6) state
7) hesitant & decisive
8) sweet & dessert
9) BU
10) way & ward

Answers

Test 11
1) fiend
2) 5
3) 32
4) BAD
5) 871975
6) N
7) mount & climb
8) hospital & school
9) C
10) SONG

Test 12
1) P
2) 47
3) sailor & drifted (lord)
4) PP
5) UPSET
6) tales
7) lenient & severe
8) silver & gold
9) OM
10) per & fume

Test 13
1) east
2) steady & unstable
3) boil & heat
4) YO
5) break & through
6) P
7) 125
8) the & alarm (heal)
9) KI
10) BOUND

Test 14
1) N
2) mystery & puzzle
3) start & dear

4) C
5) UXIXPR
6) scare
7) 13
8) 45
9) LID
10) MOTHER

Test 15
1) L
2) 33
3) live & inside (vein)
4) GL
5) ROW
6) came
7) seldom & often
8) begin & start
9) OU
10) short & age

Test 16
1) T
2) remedy & cure
3) choose & shift
4) A
5) MINER
6) trade
7) 15
8) 51
9) PEN
10) CREASE

Test 17
1) leads
2) 11
3) 10
4) ALL
5) 978254
6) C
7) divide & split
8) drake & cockerel

9) E
10) POST

Test 18
1) R
2) 9
3) piano & teacher (note)
4) OI
5) EXPRESS
6) teas
7) illegal & lawful
8) mislead & fool
9) MS
10) mouth & piece

Test 19
1) shove
2) 20
3) 31
4) OWN
5) 68813
6) E
7) disperse & scatter
8) main & pause
9) B
10) BEAR

Test 20
1) G
2) 46
3) baker & baked (kerb)
4) QG
5) MOULD
6) tear
7) destroy & create
8) scarf & close
9) PR
10) puff & in

PROGRESS CHARTS

Test	Mark	%
1		
2		
3		
4		
5		
6		
7		
8		
9		
10		
11		
12		
13		
14		
15		
16		
17		
18		
19		
20		

CERTIFICATE OF

ACHIEVEMENT

This certifies

_____

has successfully completed

11+ Verbal Reasoning
Year 5–7 GL & Other Styles
TESTBOOK 5

Overall percentage
score achieved

%

Comment _____

_____

Signed _____

(teacher/parent/guardian)

Date _____